Deserts

PEOPLE
& PLACES
IN PERIL

General Editor:
Alexander Goldsmith

Deserts

BY MARTIN JENKINS

Photographs by Still Pictures

CHERRYTREE BOOKS

Photographs supplied by
Still Pictures, except for the following:
Royal Geographical Society pp 14-15
Science Photo Library pp 36-37
ZEFA Picture Library pp 20, 21, 24-25, 38

A Cherrytree Book

Edited and produced by
Philip Clark Ltd
53 Calton Avenue
London SE21 7DF

Designed and typeset by
Hans Verkroost

Map by
European Map Graphics Ltd

First published 1995
by Cherrytree Press Ltd
a subsidiary of
The Chivers Company Ltd
Windsor Bridge Road, Bath
Avon BA2 3AX

Copyright © Cherrytree Press Ltd 1995

British Library Cataloguing in Publication Data
Jenkins, Martin
    Deserts. — (People & Places in Peril Series)
    I. Title II. Series
    304.209154

ISBN 0-7451-5215-5

Printed and bound in Italy by L.E.G.O. s.p.a., Vicenza

CONTENTS

THE DESERT WORLD

Deserts are never the sterile, lifeless expanses that many people imagine. Plants and animals have adapted themselves to even the most hostile situations, and so have humans. Since prehistoric times, people have made their homes in every desert on Earth. In fact, some of the oldest known human remains come from desert areas.

Deserts cover more than a third of the world's land. Today, more than one in ten of the world's population live in deserts. In some parts of the world, there are people who lived until quite recently much as the early desert dwellers did. A large number still carry on a traditional nomadic life, moving from place to place with their animals, homes and belongings.

Life in the desert is harsh. Food and water are hard to find. But desert people developed ingenious ways of making the best of the scarce resources. They earned a hard but sufficient living from the natural bounty of the desert.

Deserts in the Modern World

Today, the influence of the modern world has extended even to deserts. New uses have been found for arid lands: mining, tourism, ranching and even agriculture. Such change has in turn affected the lives of traditional desert peoples.

But deserts are fragile places. If change is to occur, it must take place in such a way that we do not destroy the very thing we are exploiting. Desert people, with their age-old experience of life in these harsh environments, can guide us in this quest.

Right: Sand dunes in Niger in the Sahara. Sand dunes cover about one fifth of the total area of the world's deserts. They can range in size from small ridges less than one metre (3ft) high to enormous hills of sand over 350m (1200ft) tall and 800m (half a mile) across. In some deserts, particularly the Sahara and the Arabian deserts, these dunes are gathered together in enormous seas of sand, called ergs. Very little lives in these ergs, which are some of the most barren places on Earth.

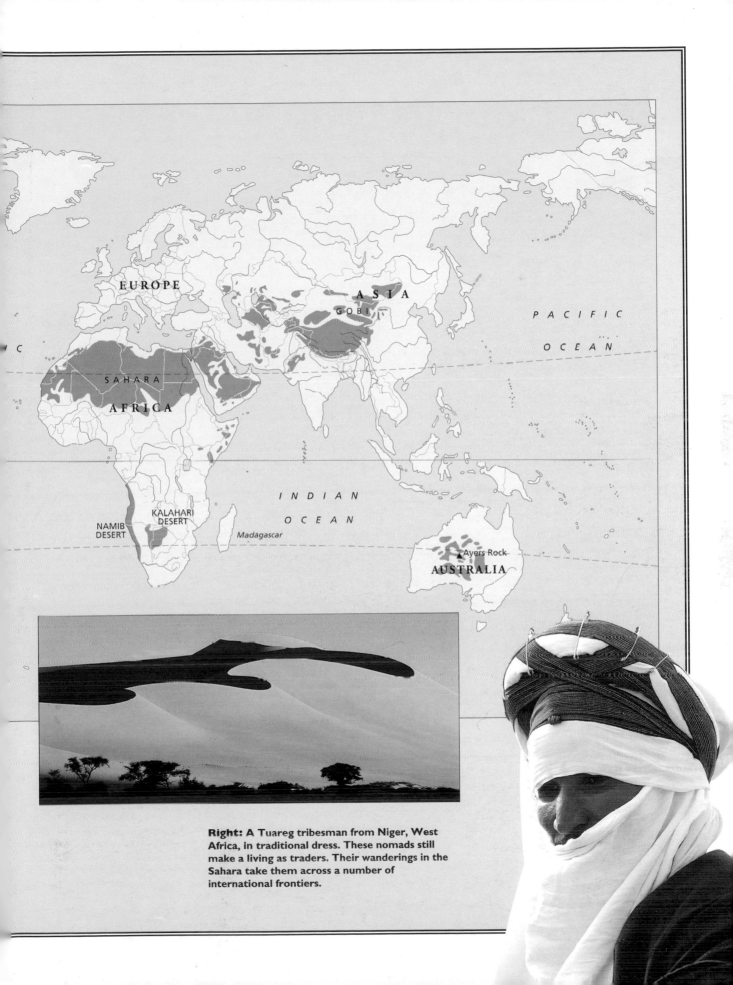

EUROPE

ASIA

GOBI

PACIFIC

OCEAN

SAHARA

AFRICA

INDIAN

OCEAN

NAMIB
DESERT

KALAHARI
DESERT

Madagascar

Ayers Rock

AUSTRALIA

Right: A Tuareg tribesman from Niger, West
Africa, in traditional dress. These nomads still
make a living as traders. Their wanderings in the
Sahara take them across a number of
international frontiers.

TYPES OF DESERT

Deserts all have one thing in common – a shortage of water. In all deserts, there is little precipitation (rain, snow and hail) or other water in the form of dew, frost and fog. Desert animals, plants and people have to adapt to this shortage. When the water does come, it is usually very irregular and unpredictable. In some areas there may be no rainfall for years on end. Then, several centimetres may suddenly fall in less than 24 hours.

Desert Variety

Although they are all dry, deserts can be very different in other ways. They may be largely sandy, or stony, or covered in pebbles. They may be flat and featureless, or rolling and hilly. They may be full of cliffs and canyons and strange rock formations. There are deserts below sea level, like Death Valley in California in the USA. There are also deserts high up on plateaus and in mountains, like the Chihuahua Desert in Mexico and the Tibetan Plateau desert, most of which is more than 4500m (about 15,000ft) above sea level.

Many deserts lie in the middle of continents, a long way from the coast. However, some, like the Atacama Desert in northern Chile and southern Peru, and the Namib Desert in southern Africa, run right down to the sea. These sea-shore deserts are some of the driest places on Earth despite being right next to the ocean.

Desert Climate

Because of this great variety, deserts can have quite different climates. We usually think of them as hot

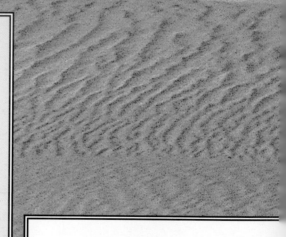

SHAPING THE LAND

The surface of the desert is constantly being eroded (worn away) by the action of wind and water. Water, when it comes, can carve

The Sahara is many people's idea of a typical desert. It is the largest desert in the world and probably the hottest. Certainly, the hottest surface temperature ever recorded (58° C/136°F) was in the Sahara, in Libya.

places, but this is not always the case. It is true that the hottest places on Earth are in deserts, but they can also be very cold. Even hot deserts like the Sahara can get surprisingly cold at night. This is because there is often little cloud cover and very little vegetation.

In other places, clouds and vegetation help to trap the sun's heat and stop the air cooling off too much at night. Mountain deserts, such as the Tibetan Plateau, remain freezing all day long in the wintertime and often stay cool during the day even at the height of summer.

The Namib Fog Desert

The Namib Desert runs for more than 1200km (750 miles) along the Atlantic coast of Namibia in southern Africa. Its northern part is called the Skeleton Coast. Often it does not rain here for years on end. Instead, for 60 to 80 days of the year, a wet fog rolls in from the Atlantic Ocean during the early morning. This fog leaves behind a heavy dew, from which the desert plants and animals obtain the water they need.

The Spiny Desert of Madagascar

Madagascar is a large island in the Indian Ocean off the south-east coast of Africa. It has been isolated from the rest of the world for tens of millions of years, so many of the animals and plants are found nowhere else. Parts of south-west Madagascar are covered in spiny desert vegetation. Sadly, the spiny desert is being destroyed at a very rapid rate as plants are cut down to make charcoal or to clear the land for cattle-grazing.

through hard rock, or leave large deposits of sediment where mountains meet plains. The Grand Canyon in the USA was formed by the Colorado River wearing away the desert surface over millions of years. Erosion by water is a powerful force in deserts as there is little vegetation to stabilize and protect the soil.

Much of the sand in deserts results from sediments eroded by water and picked up by the wind. Sediment-laden winds become strong erosion agents themselves, like the sand-blasters used to clean buildings. Small particles carried by the wind grind away at rock surfaces, forming strange wind-sculpted shapes, like this rock formation in the Sahara in Algeria.

DESERT PLANTS

Like most creatures that have become adapted to the extreme weather conditions of deserts, plants have evolved ways of coping with the shortage of water. Perhaps the most familiar desert plants are the succulents, which store water to carry them through periods with no rain.

The best-known succulents are from the cactus family. Cacti usually have thickened stems and no leaves, and are covered with a mass of thorns and prickles. The stems store water and the prickles protect the plants from being eaten by large animals. Often, cacti have roots that do not grow deep in the ground but which are spread over a very wide area. This means that when it does rain the plants can catch as much water as possible.

There are succulents with thickened stems which look very like cacti, but in fact belong to other plant families. Others store water in thickened leaves or have large, swollen underground tubers. Many desert plants, particularly trees, have roots that go down very deep where they tap underground sources of water. Since they do not have to store water themselves, they do not usually have swollen leaves or stems.

The Desert in Bloom

A number of plants, called ephemerals, have found a different way of avoiding the drought. They spend most of their lives as seeds lying on or just below the desert surface. The seeds have hard outer casings and are very resistant to heat. They can remain alive but dormant for years on end, until there is heavy rainfall. Then they sprout, grow, flower, produce more seeds and die, all in the few weeks it takes for the ground to dry out again. Usually many different species of plant do this at once. Then, the desert transforms itself, almost overnight, from a barren, brown landscape to an amazing multi-coloured carpet of flowers spreading for miles in all directions.

Right: A welwitschia in the Namib Desert. Welwitschia is a very primitive plant, related to pine trees and other conifers, but which looks like nothing else on Earth. It only ever produces two leaves which grow longer and longer, usually splitting along their length as they do so. A large welwitschia, which may be many hundreds of years old, looks more like a stranded sea-monster than a plant. Like many other plants in the Namib Desert, welwitschia gets its water from the sea-fogs.

Above: Plants in the Arizona Desert, south-western USA. Rain rarely comes to desert areas, but when it does, the desert blooms. Many desert plants have only a few weeks in which to grow, flower and re-seed themselves. They might have years to wait before the next rain falls. Their seeds are specially adapted to survive for years, awaiting their chance to flower.

THE CACTUS RUSTLERS

Because of their popularity, cacti and other succulents are sought after by people to decorate their gardens and buildings. But many of these plants are so rare and fragile that they are protected by law. Nevertheless, in the USA and other parts of the world, some people make their living by 'cactus rustling' — illegally digging up cacti at night and smuggling them out of the desert in lorries.

Some people in cities such as Los Angeles or Palm Springs will pay up to $5000 for a giant Saguaro cactus, which may be three metres (ten ft) tall. Not surprisingly, cacti like these often die after being dug up and the rustlers are kept constantly busy finding replacements. A big cactus may be several hundred years old when it is dug up, making it practically irreplaceable if it dies.

It is not just big spectacular plants like the Saguaro that are threatened by people. In many parts of the world there are keen collectors of cacti and succulents who aim to grow as many rare sorts as possible. Although nowadays most of these can be raised from seed or cuttings in nurseries, some people still prefer to own plants that have been taken from the wild. Plants from the southern USA, Mexico, southern Africa and Madagascar are particularly popular. Some of them are very rare in the wild and have only ever been found in one or two places. This makes them even more desirable to collectors, but it also means that they can easily become extinct if too many are taken. Many of them are small and even slower-growing than Saguaros. One the size of a tea-plate may be over 100 years old.

Most of these rare plants are protected by law in the countries where they grow, but it is very difficult to stop people from collecting them. The small ones especially are quite easy to smuggle out in suitcases, or even in the mail, to countries like Britain, Germany and Japan where collectors will pay large sums of money for them. Already at least one type of Mexican cactus is thought to have become extinct in the wild because of this trade.

Above: A large cactus in the southern USA. Apart from one species which lives in forests in Africa, cacti all originate from North and South America and the Caribbean. However several types, particularly prickly pears, have become wild in other parts of the world, and have become something of a menace in countries such as Australia and Madagascar.

Right: Wild millet growing in the Sahara. This grain thrives in very dry areas. It is grown in many parts of Africa as a cereal crop, but is much less often found growing wild.

DESERT ANIMALS

Like the plants, desert animals have evolved different ways of coping with the heat and shortage of water. Many of them stay in burrows underground during the day, only coming out at night when it is cool. Animals like antelopes, which are too big to make burrows, seek out every scrap of shade to shelter in during the hottest part of the day. Even a shallow depression in the ground may be enough to keep off the worst of the sun.

Below: A fennec fox in its burrow in the Sahara. Like many desert animals, fennec foxes are nocturnal, coming out to hunt at night and staying in their cool burrows during the day. They have very sharp hearing and use it to track down the beetles, grasshoppers, lizards and small mammals on which they depend. Fennec foxes' large ears also help them lose heat.

Above: A moloch or thorny devil. This fearsome-looking beast is in fact a lizard only about 15cm (6ins) long. It lives in deserts in Australia. It feeds on ants and its armoured spikes deter predators that might be tempted to eat it. Its brown and yellow colouring can also help to disguise it on the sands and pebbles of the desert surface. The moloch's body temperature, like that of other reptiles, depends on the temperature of the air. During the night when the air is cool, the lizard's body temperature drops and it becomes very sluggish. At dawn it moves out into the sun and warms up. It then becomes active during the day, although it usually shelters in the shade at midday. At this time the sun is too hot even for the moloch.

Dealing with Drought

Most desert animals can survive on much less water than other animals. Many of them do not need to drink at all, but get all the water they need from their food. Others need to drink occasionally, perhaps once a week or so. These are usually larger mammals, such as some gazelles and wild goats, and birds. They often have to travel considerable distances to find water at isolated springs and waterholes.

Ground Heat

Animals that do venture out during the day have to be able to cope with the intense heat of the ground, which can be far hotter than the air. The sand cat, which lives in deserts in North Africa and the Middle East, has hairy pads on its feet. These insulate it from the hot ground, and also allow it to keep a better grip on the sandy dunes where it lives. The sidewinder rattlesnake from North America loops sideways across the sand, only keeping a small part of its belly in contact with the ground at any one time. Some South African lizards stand on three, or even two legs, keeping the others held above the ground and constantly swapping them over. At first glance it looks as if they are performing exercises or a strange, slow dance!

Left: A scarab beetle. Many types of beetles and other insects live in deserts. Their hard outer skin helps them to conserve water and their small size means that they easily find shelter from the heat of the sun. Scarab beetles usually feed on vegetation and dung although some of them will also eat carrion — the remains of dead animals. They are an important part of the diet of many larger desert animals, including fennec foxes and other mammals.

THE LIVES OF DESERT PEOPLE

We tend to undervalue the contribution that desert people have made to our culture. Some of the world's great religions took root in these arid lands. For the spiritually-minded, the desert has always been a place of purity. A spell in the desert was regarded as an occasion for sacred renewal as well as a test of the strength of a person's religious beliefs.

In ancient days, deserts formed almost impassable barriers between different civilizations. What little contact there was resulted from the help and guidance given to travellers by desert dwellers. All contact between China and Europe before the 15th century was through desert caravans which travelled the famous Silk Road across the Gobi.

Politically, too, some desert people have wielded enormous influence. The terrifying conquests of Genghis Khan's nomadic hordes founded a massive empire that dominated central Asia for centuries.

Traditional life in deserts is a testament to the ingenuity of their inhabitants. From the most hostile conditions, human beings fashioned out a life that was plentiful, both materially and culturally.

Traditional knowledge was handed down through the generations by desert dwellers. As a result, their way of life continued almost unchanged for hundreds and sometimes thousands of years.

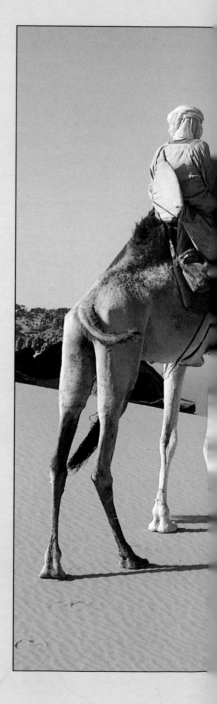

LIVING IN THE DESERT

Life has a tenuous hold on desert regions. Plants, animals and water can be found, but they are scattered over huge areas. People in desert areas have to adopt a similar strategy if they are to survive. Traditional desert life, in many parts of the world, is nomadic. To make the best of the scarce resources, desert people have to travel over great distances, taking care never to exhaust or destroy a particular resource.

Some desert dwellers live by hunting and gathering. Small groups of people range over large distances, living off the varied wild resources of the desert. The Bushmen of the Kalahari Desert and the Australian Aborigines are typical hunter-gatherers.

Pastoral nomadism is more complex. This way of life involves keeping large herds of animals, usually camels, sheep or goats, and grazing them on the desert vegetation. In some places on the edges of deserts cattle are kept too, but they are not well suited to life in real deserts.

Portable Homes
Because they have beasts of burden, pastoral nomads can carry much more than hunter-gatherers. They can carry everything they need, including their homes. These are almost always tents, made out of tightly woven wool or animal skins, supported on a wooden frame and held in place by guy-ropes. As they wander over large distances, pastoral nomads maintain good contacts with settled communities. They trade products like milk and cheese for goods that they cannot make themselves, such as pots and pans.

Permanent Settlements
Not all desert peoples are nomadic. In places were water is available all the year round, permanent settlements have grown up. The people in these settlements have built more permanent homes.

The earliest permanent homes in deserts were caves. Caves were used by people in the northern part of the Sahara and by the Pueblo Indians in the south-west of the USA. The Pueblo Indians built their cave towns over 1000 years ago. Their descendants are the Navajo

DESERT HOMES

Because few trees grow in deserts, there is almost always a severe shortage of wood, so people use stone, or baked mud or clay to build permanent dwellings.

In North Africa and in the Arabian Peninsula, whole cities have been made out of baked clay, with buildings several storeys high. These buildings would not survive for very long in wet climates, as the rain would gradually dissolve them, but in dry areas they can remain standing for centuries, and can easily be repaired if they are damaged by storms.

Desert homes usually have thick walls and small windows and doors to protect the interiors from the heat of the day and the chill of the night. In a similar way, people who live in deserts usually wear special clothing to protect themselves from the elements.

Right: A high summer camp in western Mongolia. The nomads live in tents called gers while their yaks graze nearby. Gers are made of hides and canvas wrapped around a circular wooden frame. Easy to transport and assemble, gers are also totally windproof.

Left: A mosque built from mud in Mali, western Sahara. Mud buildings, which would not last long in rainy countries, can endure for centuries in desert climates.

Below: A nomad tent, made from skins, in the Sahara near Timbuktu. Now in the modern state of Mali, the name of this town is still synonymous with the middle of nowhere.

Indians who until very recently still lived in much the same way as their ancestors. Like so many other desert peoples, their traditions have declined during the 20th century.

Desert Clothing

Daytime temperatures in the Sahara and the Arabian Peninsula can be well over 40° C (100° F). People in these areas wear long loose robes which cover their whole bodies, and often their heads as well. These clothes protect them from the blazing sun, but allow air to circulate underneath to help them keep cool.

Further south, where temperatures are not so extreme, desert dwellers wear fewer clothes. The Bushmen of the Kalahari wear next to nothing, and the Australian Aborigines wear very little. Their bodies are well adapted to heat and sunshine, although they usually avoid the hottest parts of the day. They are also very tolerant of the cold at night, although they sometimes wrap themselves in skins or lie next to their hunting dogs to keep warm.

In cold areas, such as the Gobi in Mongolia, people wear many layers of tightly-woven woollen cloth and thick animal furs to keep warm in the bitter winds that howl across the plains.

PEOPLE OF THE KALAHARI

Of all deserts, the Kalahari offers the least hostile conditions for humans. Water is never far below the surface. Although clearly a desert, the Kalahari supports plenty of savannah vegetation. With its trees, bushes and grasses, it looks not unlike parkland. A few patches of the desert are even forested.

The Kalahari is famous for its Bushmen inhabitants, a people whose way of life had until recently changed little since the Stone Age. They are quite short in stature. The men are about 150cm (5ft) tall on average and the women are slightly shorter. They speak a number of remarkable 'click' languages that contain sounds which are very difficult for westerners to imitate.

Hunter-gatherers

Bushmen once ranged all over southern Africa but their lands were gradually reduced by Bantu herding people. During the 1800s, they were hunted down by Dutch settlers who wanted their lands. They took refuge in the Kalahari, living off the land by hunting and gathering.

Of the 55,000 or so Bushmen who live in the region today, very few still live by hunting and gathering. By all accounts, their traditional way of life, though simple, was a rewarding one. Bushmen travelled in small bands of 25

Above: A prehistoric rock engraving of a giraffe by Bushmen in Namibia, Africa.

Right: These Bushmen have been turned off their traditional land. They have to do farm work for low wages in order to have enough to eat. They do not adapt well to the western way of life, and social problems often result.

Left: An elderly Bushman sucks nourishment from a root. Bushmen depend on a huge variety of plants and animals for their diet. This was generally much better than many people assume. As long as they survived the vulnerable years of their infancy, most Bushman children would grow up into healthy and fit adults.

Above: Digging for roots and tubers. These play an important part in the Bushmen's diet, and are also a source of water. The task of gathering plants was generally done by the women of the group, while the men hunted wild animals.

or so, made up of small family groups. Their food came from hunting all kinds of wild animals, and gathering berries, fruit, nuts and tubers. They travelled widely, ranging over areas of up to 1000 square kilometres (about 400 square miles).

Travelling Light

With so far to travel and no pack animals, they carried few possessions. What they did have included weapons such as wooden spears and bows and arrows. They also had bowls made of wood or plaited bark for gathering berries, and sometimes water-bags made from animal skins. Their clothes were usually also made from skins.

If they needed shelter, they used tree branches covered with bark, twigs or grass, or they spent the night in a cave or under a rock overhang. They had an extraordinary knowledge of the land, and were experts at tracking game and finding water. They sometimes stored water in empty ostrich-egg shells that they hid in the sand. During the Kalahari winter, the Bushmen would sometimes make rather more permanent wood and grass huts in which they remained for several weeks, temporarily abandoning their nomadic lifestyle.

Hunting

Usually, the men would do the hunting, tracking down animals and approaching as near as possible before shooting them with poison-tipped arrows. The women collected the berries, which formed in fact the most important part of their diet. Studies of Bushman bands have shown that their diet was extremely good and their food obtained with little effort. Their plentiful spare time was filled up with chatting, singing and dancing, or listening to their traditional myths, recounted by master story-tellers around their camp fires.

Twentieth-century Problems

Sadly, even today, people want Bushman land for cattle-ranching and mining. There are now only 2000 or so Bushmen who still live in the Kalahari region in the same way that their ancestors did. Many of the Bushmen have now settled in townships. The lure of permanent water can be irresistible. But hunter-gatherers find the modern world bewildering. Divorced from their lands and their traditional activities, they develop serious social problems, such as alcoholism.

ABORIGINES OF AUSTRALIA

In many ways, the life of the Australian Aborigines was similar to that of the Bushmen. Until British colonists arrived in Australia in the 18th century, aboriginal people lived throughout the continent, mostly in the coastal regions where the climate was more moderate than in the great arid interior. Nevertheless, a number of tribes eked out a living in these desert areas.

True Nomads

The Aborigines of the desert were truly nomadic, wandering over large areas in small groups. Like the Bushmen, they survived by hunting wild animals and collecting fruit, tubers and other edible plant matter. Again like the Bushmen, it was normally the men who did the hunting and the women who gathered the plants.

On their travels, the Aborigines carried very little — usually just weapons such as spears and boomerangs, and a few tools made of wood, stone or bone. The most important of these was a hard sharp-pointed digging stick, which the women would use for digging up tubers and sometimes as a weapon to defend themselves. Bigger implements, such as grinding stones, would be left at campsites to be used when their wanderings brought them back to the same place.

Above: Rock painting by the Wadaman people, Australia. Paintings and engravings by Australian aboriginal peoples date back tens of thousands of years. Most of them depict people, as well as the animals they hunted and mysterious figures which were probably magical spirits.

Right: Apart from its uses for cooking and providing warmth, fire is an important resource for Aborigines. Here, a hunter uses a fire to harden the points of his wooden spears. Huge bush fires are also sometimes lit to flush out game and to revive the vegetation.

Protection from the Heat

Until westerners arrived, the Aborigines generally went naked. Their dark skins protected them from sunburn and their bodies were remarkably tolerant of both the heat of the desert day and the cool of the night. Nevertheless they would seek the shade of an overhanging rock or tree during the hottest part of the day and use camp fires and blankets of tree bark to keep warm on cold nights. Occasionally, several bands would come together to form a large gathering called a 'corroboree' in which much music-making, dancing and story-telling would take place.

Aborigine Art

The Aborigines also developed sophisticated decorative art. Their elaborate abstract paintings, inspired by ancient cave paintings 35,000 years old, are a means of connecting with the 'Dreamtime', which for them is the period when all life began. These paintings are now collected the world over. Some modern aboriginal paintings sell for large sums of money.

Aborigines Today

For Aborigines, contact with white settlers has been disastrous. In the past, like the Bushmen, they were treated little better than wild animals, to be hunted down and shot. Otherwise, they were encouraged to abandon their nomadic life. Then, divorced from their past but with no role in the white man's world, they became social misfits.

Today, after decades of suffering, Aborigines have begun to redress a few of the injustices done to them. The Australian government has grudgingly accepted claims to land that is important to them for spiritual and cultural reasons, and has given them more control in deciding their own affairs. The Aboriginal Development Commission now has an all-aboriginal board of directors and receives over A$80 million every year for housing, low-cost loans, and enterprise schemes. Some 2000 aboriginal organizations receive government help.

Uluru, or Ayers Rock (see also pages 38-39), is the largest single piece of stone in the world. It is of enormous spiritual importance to the Aborigines. As one of Australia's principal tourist attractions, it is also of importance to the white majority. But now Uluru belongs once more to the Aborigines.

Above: A group of Aborigines at a corroboree. This is a gathering which involves story-telling, music and dancing. Corroborees did not normally last for very long but were important for maintaining friendships and allegiances between the smaller groups. Aborigines have a vivid imagination and a fine dramatic sense.

TUAREG PEOPLE OF THE SAHARA

Below: A veiled Tuareg youth rides a camel in the Sahara. The Tuareg refer to themselves as *Kel Taligmust*, or 'the People of the Veil'.

The largest desert in the world, the Sahara stretches for 7040 kilometres (4375 miles) from east to west and 2513 kilometres (1562 miles) north to south. It is a land shared by 11 nation states and many peoples, including Berbers, Dogon and Wodaabe. Foremost among such peoples are the Tuareg, a nomadic tribe numbering about one million individuals, whose menfolk often wear a distinctive blue veil.

The Tuareg are the most ancient inhabitants of the Sahara, although no one knows from where they came. For centuries, they have practised a nomadic or semi-nomadic way of life, raising and living off camels, goats, sheep and cattle in the central Saharan region. Through their intimate knowledge of navigating the desert, the Tuareg controlled the cross-Saharan trade – a position they sometimes abused. Riding their swift camels, Tuaregs would raid trade caravans. From the 1890s, Tuaregs began to extract salt from the desert, using it to trade for grain.

Although Tuaregs are divided into several groups and scattered over a wide area, they all speak the same language and share a common cultural heritage. Initially reluctant to adopt Islam when the new religion spread to the region in the 7th and 8th centuries, they are now devout Muslims.

Tuareg Society

Tuareg society is divided into nobles, vassals and slaves. The nobles controlled the caravan routes, the vassals were the herders and the slaves grew crops and did menial work, such as saddling the camels. In spite of this, the Tuareg are not a submissive people. They are proud, independent and egalitarian. It is said that no Tuareg kneels when his chief passes and, indeed, the chief is removable at any time.

Like other desert people, modern life has brought difficulties for the Tuareg. Their traditional activities have come under increasing strain.

Above: A Tuareg family outside their grass hut. People from this nomadic tribe still make a living as traders.

Below: Traditional and modern combine at a Tuareg wedding ceremony. Guests carry wedding presents of radio cassette players.

Above: A Tuareg woman filling camel-hide waterskins at a well.

Air transport has replaced the caravan. Their salt is no longer wanted and their grazing lands have been gradually taken away. Tuareg territory cuts across the boundaries of six newly-independent nation-states: Mali, Burkina Faso, Mauritania, Niger, Algeria and Libya. Their independent spirit has brought them into conflict with these states, and it is likely that a low-intensity guerrilla war will continue until the Tuareg feel they have their freedom.

DESERT PEOPLE OF NORTH AMERICA

The settlement of the American continent by Europeans marked the beginning of a tragic age for the indigenous peoples. For most of the original inhabitants of the north and south alike, contact with settlers spelt the end of their way of life.

The desert tribes of the North American south-west, however, fared slightly better than Plains Indian tribes like the Sioux and the Cree or the Aztec and Inca civilizations of Central and South America. The tough, arid terrain inhabited by the Hopi Indians of Arizona (and their neighbours, the Navajo) held fewer attractions for European colonists.

The Hopi lived in clifftop villages in densely-packed houses built of stone and rendered with clay. For defence, few of the houses had doors. Instead, ladders were used to climb onto the roofs, from which the rooms could be entered. The Hopi farmed corn and the crop formed a central part of their culture and religious life. 'Corn is the heart of the Hopi' went the local proverb.

The Navajo

By contrast, the Navajo were mainly a hunting and gathering people and lived in more scattered communities than the Hopi. As fierce fighters, they

Above: Tourists visit Cliff Palace at Mesa Verde, Colorado, USA. These cliff dwellings, probably designed for defence, were used by the Anasazi people from the 1100s to the 1300s. ('Anasazi' was a Navajo word meaning 'enemy'.)

raided the more peaceable Hopis for food and goods. In winter, they inhabited 'hogans', small one-roomed houses that were also central to their religious lives since it was in these structures that they performed their healing ceremonies. Navajo were skilled jewellers, working mainly with silver and turquoise. Navajo-style jewellery is today a popular fashion accessory.

Although contact with the Europeans was less traumatic than in other parts of the New World, it happened nevertheless. The Spanish invaders tried to impose the Catholic faith on the Hopi, who rebelled. Many Hopi fled to live with the Navajo and, over time, the two groups adopted each other's customs.

Today, the Navajo are the largest Indian group in the US, numbering about 150,000. They live on the Navajo Reservation, which occupies land in Arizona, New Mexico and Utah. They herd sheep and goats, although the land is heavily overgrazed. Some Navajo make a living from weaving blankets and making jewellery. In spite of this, there is chronic unemployment and widespread social problems.

COLD DESERTS OF ASIA

There are several desert regions in Asia, but the largest and best-known is the Gobi. This is made up of several distinct arid regions which stretch across south-east Mongolia and northern China. The fifth largest desert area in the world, it is also one of the most hostile, with temperatures as low as minus 40 °C (minus 40 °F) in winter and as high as 45 °C (113 °F) in summer. The word 'Gobi' is derived from the Mongolian word for waterless place.

The semi-nomadic Khalkha Mongols make up the largest tribal group in the Gobi. They herd sheep and goats, although their mainstay is the Bactrian, or two-humped, camel. There are 600,000 of these animals in the Gobi. They provide their owners with many of their needs: meat, milk, wool, hides for tents and dung for fuel. In addition, the Bactrian camel is an extremely hardy beast of burden, capable of carrying 200 kilogrammes (440 pounds) for long distances under extreme conditions.

The nomads of the Gobi live in circular, domed tents called 'gers', which are made of many layers of skins and cloth tied over a wooden frame. The layers of material provide good insulation against freezing temperatures.

Above: Mongols in the southern Gobi. The celebration of the first mare's milk of the year is combined with a hair-cutting ceremony. There are 17 families represented here. The guests are in their best clothes, having arrived on horseback and by motorbike. Tea is being served.

Below: A herdsboy in central Mongolia brings in calves for the night. In the background are huge sand dunes.

Above: A Mongol family in their ger, which is decorated with brightly-coloured rugs. The word yurt is sometimes also used for the tent, but strictly speaking it refers both to the tent and its accompanying enclosure.

BACTRIAN CAMEL

A bactrian camel in south-central Gobi, Mongolia. The camel — the so-called 'Ship of the Desert' — is truly a wonderful, if notoriously grumpy, animal. It can go for days without water, although it does not actually store any in its hump. It can survive on the coarse vegetation of desert areas and can walk for miles through the hot sun without becoming overheated. Its broad flat feet stop it sinking into the soft sand and its long eyelashes and special nostril-flaps keep sand and grit out of its eyes and nose during sandstorms. It supplies the desert people with milk and meat, hair for weaving into cloth, skin for tents and bags and transport for people and their belongings.

Uses and Abuses of Deserts

Deserts provide a living for large numbers of people as well as many benefits for those who live far away. Deserts are fragile places, however, and can easily be abused. Traditional desert people learned over the years how much they could take out of the land without destroying it. But in recent years, this situation has changed dramatically.

Aircraft and four-wheel-drive vehicles have placed even the most remote areas of desert within the reach of humans. Indigenous desert dwellers now find themselves in the company of tourists, hunters, soldiers, traders and mineral prospectors. In their different ways, all these newcomers affect the desert environment, either through sheer weight of numbers or because of the activities they are engaged in. Also, newcomers to desert areas often do not understand how deserts work.

The traditional inhabitants of deserts have changed too. Their populations have increased greatly, placing more and more pressure on the land. The digging of new boreholes and wells encourages people to keep more livestock which may overgraze the land around the wells, causing erosion. Such problems will need to be overcome both to preserve what is of value in desert environments and to prevent the desert from encroaching on less arid regions.

Below: Cattle at a waterhole in Niger. Although cattle are not well adapted to living in true deserts, they are traditionally kept in large numbers in semi-desert areas, such as here in the Sahel, the dry region to the south of the Sahara in North Africa. The tribes which keep cattle are nomadic, like many true desert people. They keep moving with their herds to areas where it has just rained and where there is new growth of grasses for grazing.

Right: Modern 'nomads' in the Nevada Desert in the USA. Good roads and mobile homes have meant that people can travel more easily than ever before. In America, areas like the Nevada Desert, which were once regarded as hostile, forbidding places, are now popular destinations for tourists. Like traditional nomads, these travellers can carry their homes, food and water with them. However, unlike true nomads, most of them also have permanent homes that they can return to.

MODERN LIFE IN DESERTS

As in other areas of the world, life in deserts has been greatly changed by modern technology. You are now as likely to find a Tuareg at the wheel of a pickup truck as riding a camel. Even isolated desert communities have contact with the outside world through radios, telephones and television.

New Desert Dwellers

Modern towns in deserts are often built of imported materials such as breeze-blocks and corrugated iron rather than local clay or stone. The inhabitants of these towns are often not traditional desert dwellers. In many parts of the world, the dry climate and endless sunshine have attracted new groups of people to deserts. These include holiday-makers, retired people and workers in high-technology industries such as electronics. In the USA, the desert states in the south-west of the country are experiencing an economic boom while the old industrial centres of the north and east decline.

But, in contrast to traditional desert life, modern life in deserts uses up large amounts of energy and water, most of which has to be imported. Metal caravans and homes may be cheap and easy to move but they can become unbearably hot in the glaring sun, making air-conditioning and refrigeration a necessity. Both the new residents and tourists in desert hotels love the climate but also demand swimming pools and lush gardens to relax in. Such thirsty habits leave less and less water for other uses.

Greening the Desert

Because there is little rain, the earliest permanent human settlements in deserts were near other sources of water such as springs, or along rivers. People soon learned, however, that they could move water around to suit their needs. Over two thousand years ago, the ancient Persians built underground canals tens of kilometres long, called 'qanats', to

GREENING DESERTS

Water from a well is used to irrigate this oasis in Sudan. People have been digging wells to obtain water for centuries. More than 1000 years ago, the ancient Persians were using wells over 100m (300ft) deep. Many ingenious devices were developed for lifting water out of wells, although water from the very deepest ones had to be hauled up by bucket. These days, water from wells is still very important in desert areas. It is often extracted in ways which have not changed for hundreds of years.

Below: A modern settlement in Israel. All over the world, more and more people are coming to live in desert areas and new settlements are springing up. These new developments are usually built with conventional building materials and lack the special character of traditional desert homes.

Above: A luxury hotel in the Sinai Peninsula in Egypt. The hot, dry climate of desert areas attracts more and more holiday-makers. Tourist developments like these have brought much-needed employment to parts of the world where there were few other ways of earning a living. However, they have also brought their own problems. Hotels, swimming pools and gardens use up enormous amounts of water — the most precious commodity in deserts. Tourists also produce a great deal of waste which is difficult to get rid of in these sensitive environments.

carry water from mountain ranges into deserts to grow crops and make gardens. Similar systems are still used today in some parts of the world.

Extracting Groundwater

There are often large amounts of water deep beneath deserts. This water, called groundwater, collects in layers of porous rock known as aquifers. In some places it can be reached by sinking wells into the ground. With modern drilling equipment, people can bore wells to the deepest aquifers and extract water with mechanical pumps. They can obtain more water than ever before.

However, this advance has caused problems. A lot of the water in desert aquifers has been there for tens of thousands of years. It collected when the climate was wetter than it is now and, like desert oil, is not replaced naturally when it is taken out. Traditional systems of water extraction did not use very much, leaving enough for future generations. Modern extraction takes out very large amounts, and is often wasteful. The water is therefore being used up at a rapid rate. Already supplies have been virtually exhausted in some parts of the USA, and the same is expected to happen soon in other areas.

DESERT HUNTERS

Traditional methods gave desert hunters the means to kill animals for food and even some for sport, but not enough to wipe out an entire species. Today, all this has changed. Modern desert hunters use guns – rifles, shotguns and even machine guns – and chase animals across the desert in four-wheel-drive vehicles that can easily run down a gazelle on open ground.

Below: An Arab falconer with a saker falcon. Falconry has long been a traditional sport in the Middle East. It was once the preserve of princes and kings, but with the arrival of oil wealth in the region, more and more people have been able to take it up. This has led to a great demand for falcons, many of which are now illegally taken from the wild and smuggled out of countries in Europe, Africa and the rest of Asia.

Desert animals can make easy prey for hunters. There is little vegetation for the animals to hide in. Under stress, they easily succumb to the extreme conditions. Even if they are not shot, antelopes chased across the desert may die of heat exhaustion.

All in all, there has been a horrifying slaughter of large desert animals in the 20th century, especially in North Africa and the Middle East. Antelopes such as the scimitar-horned oryx, the addax and the Dama gazelle in the Sahara and the Arabian oryx and gazelle have been hunted to virtual extinction.

The Arabian Oryx

The Arabian oryx did indeed become extinct in the wild. Arabian oryx are beautiful creatures with long sweeping horns. Well-adapted to desert conditions, they thrived for centuries in the Arabian peninsula. But the very characteristics that helped them live in the desert made them easy prey. Arabian oryx have white coats to reflect the heat and they move slowly to stay cool. Their migrations are very predictable.

These splendid creatures were hunted to extinction in the wild in the late 1950s. In the following years, the few that survived in captivity were put through a breeding programme in an attempt to save the species from extinction. Fortunately, the Arabian oryx's desert habitat has survived, enabling it to be re-introduced into the wild in the 1980s. This project has been one of the few successful examples of its kind.

ENERGY FROM THE DESERT

Plants and animals in deserts have been exploited by people for centuries. One desert resource which has only recently begun to be exploited is energy. Its use has had a huge effect both on desert countries and on the world at large.

Oil and Natural Gas

The main source of energy from deserts is oil. Drilling for oil on a large scale started in the eastern United States in the 1860s. The industry expanded rapidly and oil prospectors spread out across the world in search of new deposits. They soon found large quantities of oil in the desert areas of the western and south-western USA and in Mexico.

At the beginning of the 20th century, the largest reserves of oil and natural gas in the world were discovered in the desert regions of the Middle East and North Africa. These have been heavily exploited since then and have brought enormous wealth and rapid modernization to many of the countries in the region. The Middle East is responsible for 25 per cent of the world's total oil production.

Above: A windmill farm in California. As well as usually being very sunny, deserts are often very windy places. In some parts of the world, people are making use of this to generate energy, using windmills to drive electric generators. Some of these windmills are very large and can generate considerable amounts of electricity. Windmill farms are being set up in other parts of the world as well as deserts. In the future, they may become an increasingly important way of generating power without causing pollution.

Left: Oilfields at El-Borma in Tunisia. The presence of oil shows that these areas were once submerged beneath the sea. The oil is the broken-down remains of tiny plants and animals that lived in the sea hundreds of millions of years ago. These remains were buried under layers of sand and mud. Under great pressure, they gradually turned into oil and natural gas. Much of this became trapped in layers of spongy rock.

Below: Luz Solar Energy Plant. Although it looks very spectacular, this solar energy plant, like most others, generates only a relatively small amount of energy. Up to now, energy from these plants has only been used in a few countries such as Israel, Jordan and the United States. Scientists and engineers are looking at ways of using it for other purposes, such as generating electricity on a large scale.

Fossil Fuel Pollution

Most countries are very dependent on the income they generate through oil sales. But oil and gas are non-renewable resources. Once they are used up, there will not be any more. Burning them also creates enormous amounts of pollution throughout the world, especially in the form of carbon dioxide and sulphur dioxide.

People everywhere are therefore starting to look for cleaner sources of energy. Two new sources which may become increasingly important in the future are solar power and wind power. Both wind and sunshine are present in large amounts in deserts. However, the technology that allows these energy sources to be harnessed economically has yet to be perfected.

DESERTS AS DUSTBINS

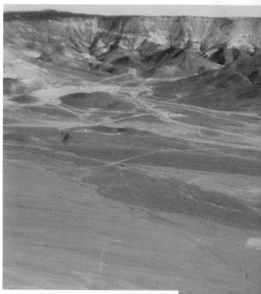

Cheap land, the absence of vegetation, and plentiful space have made deserts attractive to mining companies. Apart from fossil fuels, deserts contain a huge variety of valuable resources: iron ore, diamonds, gold, potash, phosphates and uranium. Mining companies can make use of the large open spaces with little fear of environmental protest. For this reason, deserts have suffered from activities that would not be tolerated if they were closer to large centres of population.

Above: Western travellers stop for the night in the Hoggar Mountains, near Ain Ecker, north of Tamanrasset, in the Algerian Sahara. This was the site of French overground nuclear testing in the 1950s.

Right: Sedan Crater is the result of the underground explosion of a 100 kilotonne nuclear bomb in the Nevada desert on 6 July 1962. The crater is 98m (320ft) deep and 390m (1280ft) across. The explosion displaced about 12 million tonnes of earth. The Nevada Test Site is about 65 miles (105km) north-west of Las Vegas.

Remoteness affects deserts in another respect. It helps to guarantee secrecy. For this reason, many of the world's major deserts have been used for nuclear weapons research. Indigenous desert people have invariably suffered from such uses.

Nuclear Legacies

The very first atomic bomb was detonated at 5.30 am on 16 July 1945 in the US desert near Almagordo, New Mexico. Subsequently, the US performed several dozen atmospheric nuclear tests at a desert site in Nevada. Each test would result in a heavily radioactive fallout plume that in some cases would stretch across 160km (100 miles) of desert. Hundreds more tests were carried out underground, right up to 1992, when the Cold War nuclear rivalry between the USA and the Soviet Union finally came to an end.

Testing Sites

Britain undertook a series of nuclear tests at Maralinga in the Great Victoria Desert of South Australia in the 1950s and 1960s. The site is still heavily contaminated with radioactivity. Many aboriginal people, unable to read the warning signs near the test site, unknowingly hunted and fished in the area and were exposed to radioactive fallout. One report spoke of the bodies of four Aborigines found in a bomb crater after one of the tests in 1963. Another states that the British buried some radioactive debris on an Aboriginal reserve and covered it with only a few centimetres of soil.

Most of the other big nuclear powers – France, the former Soviet Union and China – have tested their bombs in desert environments. In the 1960s, France performed 17 nuclear weapons tests in the Algerian Sahara before transferring its operations to the Pacific. India, too, exploded a nuclear bomb in the Thar Desert of Rajasthan.

Other Radioactive Threats

Nuclear weapons testing has not been the only radioactive threat to deserts. Many desert areas are rich in uranium. Uranium mining, whether for civilian or military purposes, creates a host of radioactive hazards. The US state of New Mexico, mainly desert, is dotted with uranium mines. Lands reserved for indigenous people in the north-west of the state were used by the US government to supply 25 per cent of the country's commercial and military needs.

Equally, deserts are considered suitable sites for the dumping of nuclear waste. For years now, Carlsbad in New Mexico has been under consideration for a long-term waste disposal facility.

TOURISM IN DESERTS

More and more people are travelling the world. At the same time, people are becoming more aware of unspoilt areas, and more interested in visiting them. All these factors mean that tourism is growing very quickly in the Earth's wild places, including deserts. While some tourists come only for the sun and warmth, many more visit deserts because they know that they can see some of the most beautiful places on Earth, with magnificent land forms, clear skies and a great variety of fascinating plants and animals.

Uluru (Ayers Rock), Australia

One of the most visited desert places is Uluru, or Ayers Rock, in Australia's Northern Territory. Despite being one of the most isolated places in the country, over a quarter of a million people visit the rock each year.

This influx of visitors has brought important economic benefits to the region, but has also caused a number of problems. Tourists have to be housed and fed, and their rubbish cleared away. If these jobs are not carried out carefully, there is a serious danger that development for tourism will ruin the area's natural beauty — which is the very thing that the tourists come for in the first place.

Deserts of the USA

In the western part of the USA, large numbers of tourists have for many years been visiting its famous desert sites, such as the Painted Desert and Petrified Forest in Arizona and Bryce Canyon National Park, Utah. Here, tourism is carefully controlled, especially in areas which can easily be damaged. These areas can often only be visited on foot or horseback and the number of visitors at any one time is limited. In this way, it should be possible to preserve these fragile landscapes for future generations.

Above: Uluru, formerly known as Ayers Rock, is one of the most important sacred sites for Australia's Aborigines. Nine km (five and a half miles) in circumference, it is the largest single piece of stone on the Earth's surface. Uluru is located near the centre of Australia. It is a major tourist attraction, drawing over a quarter of a million visitors each year.

Right: The rising sun is reflected from Mount Olga. This is the name of a huge group of strange-shaped rocks, not far from Uluru. In 1950, the Ayers Rock-Mount Olga area was designated the Uluru National Park.

Below: Tourists on horseback in Bryce Canyon National Park, Utah, USA.

THE FUTURE OF DESERTS

Deserts, like other environments the world over, are changing fast as a result of the actions of people. But deserts face two major threats, which seem to contradict each other. One problem is the destruction of natural deserts. The other is desertification, the changing of non-desert areas into desert.

Desertification

There is controversy over how big a threat desertification represents. For many years, scientists were particularly worried about the Sahel, a region to the south of the Sahara. It was thought that cattle were overgrazing, especially during dry years, causing the Sahara to spread southwards.

Now experts are not so sure. The problems might have been due to the prolonged drought, and the land could well return to normal once the weather has stabilized. In fact, both explanations may be correct. Land degradation in naturally arid areas, through overgrazing or the removal of tree cover, can make the environment more hostile than it already is.

Salinization, too, can leave formerly irrigated areas parched and lifeless. As irrigation water evaporates, it leaves behind salts that were dissolved in the water. Such salts can leave a crust and render the soil useless for agriculture.

Above: Sand dunes spreading in West Africa. The boundaries of deserts have always moved. However, in recent years many people have feared that they are spreading further and faster than before. These dunes in West Africa are moving forwards and killing the trees in their path.

Right: Soil erosion in deserts and semi-desert areas is a major problem. Soils in arid areas are usually very poor in quality, and are held in place by the thin covering of vegetation. If this vegetation is destroyed because too many domestic animals graze on it, or because motor vehicles drive over it too often, the soil will be blown away, or even washed away in a desert storm. Without the soil, the vegetation is unable to grow back.

DESERTS ON THE MOVE

Deserts can grow, or shrink, for several different reasons. The climate may change, or people and their animals may destroy the vegetation in areas which are dry but not quite deserts. When the vegetation goes, the soil gets washed, or blown, away. Nothing will grow, turning what was once a green area into a desert. Destroying the vegetation may even change the climate itself, so that it rains less than it did before.

Plants as Anchors

Deserts, particularly sandy ones, often move just because of the wind. Sand dunes, blown along by the wind, can travel quite quickly, burying houses, trees and crops. For many years, people have looked for ways to stop deserts spreading. One of the most important ways of doing this is to replant vegetation. The plants chosen are tough ones which will grow quickly and do not need much water. As they grow, their roots bind the soil or sand particles together and stop it from moving.

Sometimes, slow-growing plants that spread out across the ground are used. These can then provide some

Above: Stone lines being built in Burkina Faso in West Africa. Even low stone lines like these can hold the shifting sand and soil in place. They can also stop water running off when it rains. In deserts, rainfall is often sudden and very fierce. Much of the water runs off into dry stream and river beds before it can soak into the ground. Stone lines like these can hold up the water long enough for it to soak in and irrigate plants.

Planting trees in Mauritania. As well as stopping erosion, trees in deserts can be very valuable for other reasons. They can provide valuable firewood and food for livestock, and form windbreaks for sheltering tents and houses. However, they need careful attention after they have been planted if they are to grow well. Often trees used in schemes to stop desertification get neglected after they have been planted. As a result, many of them die, which is very wasteful.

shade for seedlings of bigger plants, including trees, which will then send roots deeper into the ground and provide an even firmer anchor. Planting is usually done by hand. In some parts of the world, grass seed has been sown from aircraft. This method is quicker but is also much more expensive.

If the ground is eroding very quickly or sand dunes are moving too fast, stone walls or wooden fences can be used. These can hold up the moving soil for long enough to allow plants to get a firm grip. These systems are often also used on sandy beaches and in sand dunes in countries like the United Kingdom and France which have no real deserts.

DESERT PARKS

One of the most important ways in which deserts can be preserved is to make them, or at least parts of them, national parks or nature reserves. There are now many large and important parks and reserves in deserts throughout the world, some of which cover thousands of square kilometres. Sometimes the parks serve to protect beautiful or unique landscapes. Others are to preserve rare and endangered plants and animals. Of course, many combine the two functions.

Running Costs

Wealthy countries such as Australia and the USA spend a lot of money making sure their parks are properly run. The money is needed to ensure that animals and plants are not poached and to provide facilities for people who visit the parks. However, many important desert parks are in countries which do not have much money to spare. It is often difficult for governments in these countries to protect their parks completely. In many cases, people still live in the parks or reserves and it is important that their needs are met as well as those of the wild animals and plants in the area.

The Aïr and Ténéré Nature Reserve

One of the most important desert reserves is the Aïr and Ténéré Nature Reserve in Niger in the central part of the Sahara. This reserve is enormous, covering 7,736,000 hectares (nearly 20 million acres) and protects the last wild populations of two of the largest and most

Above: Monument Valley Navajo Tribal Park lies within the Navajo Indian Reservation in Utah and Arizona, USA. Although many interesting plants and animals live there, Monument Valley is best known for its wonderful landscape of eroded rocks. These are familiar to film-goers all over the world through the many Westerns that have been filmed in the valley.

WORLD HERITAGE SITES

All national parks and other protected areas are considered important by the countries that have set them up. Some of them are so special that they are regarded as important by the international scientific community. Many of these areas are given an international designation and are called World Heritage Sites. The World Heritage Convention was set up by Unesco, an agency of the United Nations, in 1972. Over 110 countries have joined the Convention and between them have declared over 300 sites as World Heritage Sites.

These sites may be natural areas which are extremely beautiful or have many endangered species of animals and plants. They may also be areas that are of great historical interest or architectural importance. The Convention can help countries that do not have much money to protect their World Heritage Sites. Many of the most famous World Heritage Sites are in desert areas. These include natural areas such as the Grand Canyon in Arizona in the USA and Uluru National Park in central Australia, as well as historical sites such as the Pyramids in Egypt and the rock temples at Petra in Jordan.

beautiful of desert animals, the addax and the scimitar-horned oryx.

The Aïr and Ténéré reserve is the last hope for them to survive in the wild, although fortunately they exist in zoos in various parts of the world. Other rare animals living in the reserve include Dama gazelles, aoudad (Barbary sheep) and cheetahs. Not many tourists visit the reserve, because it is so inaccessible. But it is hoped that the numbers will increase gradually, and that they will be able to help pay for its running costs.

Deserts are Special

People who have never been to deserts find it hard to understand their special qualities. But those who have find it hard to forget them. The fighting spirit of desert people is balanced by their unfailing hospitality to strangers. People from heavily populated areas of the world often find that visiting a desert is a moving spiritual experience.

There are many reasons why deserts should be valued and preserved. The desert environment gives shape and meaning to the lives of its people, who understand better than most how to live from it without destroying it. It harbours rare and beautiful species, uniquely adapted to the extreme conditions. But the best reason of all is also the simplest. In a crowded planet, deserts are some of the last true wildernesses.

Above: A herd of addax in the Aïr and Ténéré reserve in Niger. Like the scimitar-horned oryx, the addax was a common antelope in the Sahara until recently. It was even better adapted than the oryx to life in the very hottest and driest parts of the desert. Sadly, it too has been hunted virtually to extinction in the last 20 or 30 years. The last wild population lives in the Aïr and Ténéré reserve where it is hoped that it will survive for many years to come.

A SMALL DESERT RESERVE

Not all desert parks and reserves are large. Some small areas can be very important for tourism or for preserving rare plants and animals. One small but important reserve is the Berenty Reserve in the spiny desert in southern Madagascar. This only covers 250 hectares (600 acres) but attracts tourists and scientists from all over the world. They come especially to see the Verreaux's sifaka and ring-tailed lemurs which live there. Three other sorts of lemur are found in the reserve as well as over 70 types of bird which are only found in the Madagascar region. There is also a breeding colony of radiated tortoises.

Index and Glossary

48